THE TAROT JOURNAL

OTHER BOOKS BY CARL JAPIKSE:

Exploring the Tarot
The Light Within Us
Poems of Light
The Hour Glass
The Enlightened Management Journal
The $1.98 Cookbook
The Biggest Tax Cheat in America is the I.R.S.

as Waldo Japussy:

The Tao of Meow

with Robert R. Leichtman, M.D.:

Active Meditation
Forces of the Zodiac
The Light of Learning
Tapping Our Rich Potential
Perfecting the Emotions
Harnessing Our Noble Mind
Expanding Our Horizons
Completing the Masterpiece
The Life of Spirit
Our Spiritual Resources
The Divine Workshop
Healing Lines
Ruling Lines
Connecting Lines
Changing Lines

The Tarot Journal

by Carl Japikse

ARIEL PRESS
Atlanta, Georgia

No Royalties Are Paid on This Book

This book is made possible
by a gift from Bill & Ann Harper
to the Publications Fund of Light

THE TAROT JOURNAL
Copyright © 1999 by Light

All Rights Reserved. No part of this book may be used or reproduced in any manner whatsoever without written permission, except in the case of brief quotations embodied in articles and reviews. Printed in the United States of America. Direct inquiries to: Ariel Press, P.O. Box 297, Marble Hill, GA 30148.

ISBN 0-89804-044-2

Introduction

The Tarot is one of the best tools available to us for exploring the inner dimensions of our character and consciousness—when correctly used. I have described the intelligent use of the Tarot as an adjunct to personal and spiritual growth in my book, **Exploring the Tarot.** This new book, **The Tarot Journal,** is designed to be written by you—as you record your use of the Tarot in conducting these explorations. It is meant to become a thorough record of your own inner life, as you put the Tarot to work exploring the depths of your character and subconscious—and revising them to serve you better.

One of the greatest practices of the spiritual life is what Socrates called "the examined life"—the effort to define our personal baseline of values, convictions, beliefs, goals, and behavior. The person who has not examined the many dimensions of his consciousness is not much of an adult—even if he or she happens to be 40 or 50 years old.

Some of this self-examination occurs as we weigh the words we say and the emotions we feel. More of it is stimulated by feedback from friends and colleagues, and from the events of life itself. Dreams can occasionally be helpful in showing us inner conflicts. But even if we manage to harness all of these resources, there will still be dimensions of our consciousness that escape our purview. These are the various blind spots, bad seeds, and buried poisons that govern much of our automatic behavior—the very part of our automatic behavior that we most desire to change.

But how does anyone discover and change a blind spot—or any kind of subliminal poison? This is where the Tarot serves so neatly. The Tarot is perfectly designed to answer otherwise inscrutable questions as:

- What habit or attitude of mine impedes my spiritual growth the most?
- What quality of spirit do I most need to add to my character—and how?
- How am I making my marriage more difficult than it needs to be?
- What should I be working on in my own life in order to be a better parent?
- What changes could I make to reduce the conflict I have been experiencing with my boss?
- How can I increase the clarity of my thinking?
- What is the ideal plan for my success at college?

Please note that these are not the standard kinds of questions usually associated with the Tarot. For far too long, the Tarot has been the plaything of fortune tellers, who presume to use it to foretell cheap fortunes. This practice is an abuse of the true potential of the Tarot, however. Correctly used, the Tarot will peel back the layers of wishful thinking and selfishness that normally cloud our perception, and help us begin to view life as it is—and as it ought to be.

The Tarot is a deck of 78 cards—22 in the Major Arcana and 56 in the Minor Arcana. The 22 cards in the Major Arcana correspond to the 22 letters in the

Hebrew alphabet and the 22 paths in the Kabalah. The 56 cards in the Minor Arcana are divided into four suits of 14 cards each: swords, rods, cups, and pentacles. Pentacles are sometimes referred to as coins. Each suit resembles, superficially, the cards in a suit in a deck of ordinary playing cards, with the exception that there is a Page and a Knight in place of the solitary Jack.

There are hundreds of different Tarot decks—some quite ancient, many quite modern. I use **The Aquarian Tarot** designed by David Palladini. The Ryder-Waite deck is also quite excellent. **The Tarot Journal** can be used effectively with any legitimate Tarot deck.

Each card in the Tarot represents a divine archetypal force or design. Some are easy to discern: the card Strength, for example, represents the divine principle of strength, which must be translated into human qualities and talents such as courage, leadership, and endurance. Others are more difficult to interpret: the card Moon, for example, often represents the dead issues of past lessons that still influence our present behavior, but from unconscious levels. Until they are defined and removed, they will haunt us like ghosts.

In examining a question with the Tarot, you would begin by shuffling the full deck. Then you would lay out the first 10 cards off the top of the deck in the pattern depicted on page 8. In so doing, you create an elaborate structure of intelligence which will guide your thinking toward the proper answer. This pattern or structure consists not only of the 10 cards you have selected, but also the 10 positions where you place them in your layout. Each position represents a different aspect of your question—and its answer.

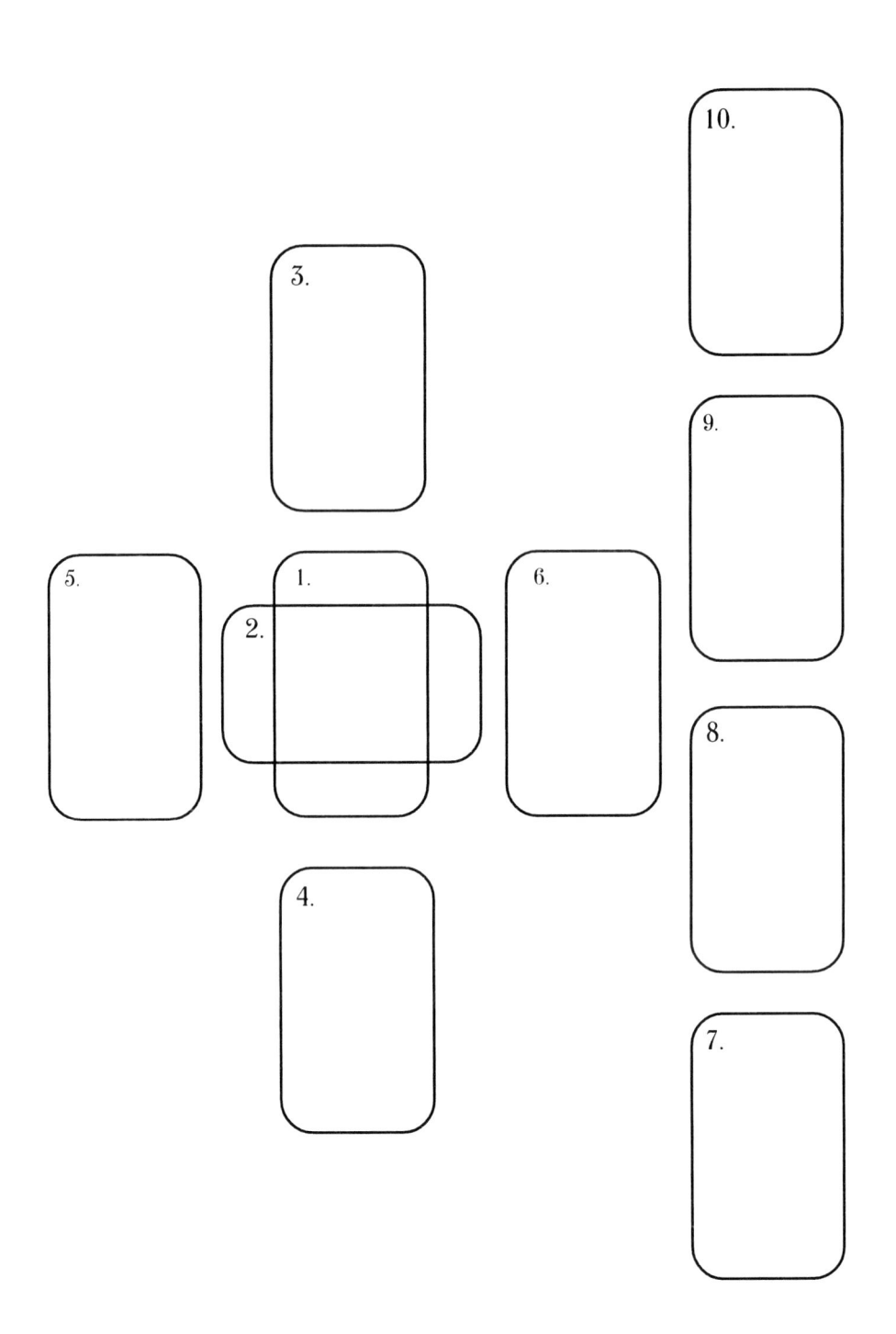

THE BASIC TAROT JOURNAL LAYOUT

The first card laid down is the **Starting Point,** which presents the problem as you have defined it—but examining it from a more holistic perspective.

The second card is the **Counterpoint,** which reveals the forces that oppose or complement the starting point. This card often suggests something you are overlooking which is part of your problem. It is laid horizontally upon the starting card, but can be removed and set below it for easier inspection.

The third card set down is the **Creative Challenge.** What is this problem or aspect of your life asking you to learn? How are you expected to grow? How can you become a better person?

The fourth card laid down is the **Purpose.** It puts your specific question in a larger context, defining the lesson to be learned from the perspective of the higher self or soul. This is an important card to remember as you fill up your journal, as it is a way of "indexing" related readings. Let's say the Nine of Cups appears four times in the 80 readings you record in this book. This would indicate that these four readings are closely linked, because they all relate to the same greater purpose. Understanding how they are related, and why, could be an important step forward in your self-understanding.

The fifth card set down is the **Endowment.** It represents the past history of your question; in specific, the skills and abilities (or the hang-ups and hurdles) that you have already acquired that will help you solve your problem (or keep you stuck in the mud).

It is complemented by the sixth card, the **Destiny.** This card indicates where this situation is heading, and what will be required of you in order to grow.

Together, these first six cards in the spread represent "The Cross of Definition"—they describe the forces and conditions actively at work creating the situation.

The final four cards, by contrast, are called "The Pillar of Revelation," because they describe the hidden forces at work, shaping the situation—and your answer.

The seventh card laid down is **The Real Question,** and it, too, is a good card to use in indexing your readings. It suggests that full understanding of your situation will only come when you have rephrased your original question more comprehensively. If your original question is "Why do people make fun of me?" and you receive the Six of Rods in this spot, it might be a suggestion to rephrase your question: "How do my attitudes and emotional outbursts alienate others from me?"

The eighth card in the layout is **Unseen Forces,** which can range anywhere from unconscious influences arising out of your own doubts and fears on the one hand to the force of public opinion on the other. If a card such as "The Hermit" came up in this spot in a reading on writing a new book or introducing a new project, for example, it could indicate that someone else is already far ahead of you in developing something similar, and will trump you in the marketplace.

The ninth card in the spread describes **The Spiritual Ideal,** and it indicates the spiritual force or law you need to pursue in order to achieve success. If the card "Justice" appeared in a question about dealing with a lying child, it would tend to indicate that this child lacks any sense of conscience and needs to be taught in no uncertain terms that the abuse of speech to mislead others leads to punishment and restriction.

The final card is **The Fulfillment**—the crowning outcome or conclusion of your question. If the final card in the previous example was the five of cups, it would indicate that the child will ignore most of your advice while a child, but some of the "spilled milk" of your wisdom will sink in and become a guiding force as an adult.

As these 10 cards are laid out, some will be right side up and some will be upside down, as the result of the normal process of shuffling and mixing. Some systems of Tarot place great importance on whether a card is upright or inverted. This kind of interpretation is left over from the fortune telling perversions of the Tarot. Beginniners ought to ignore this factor altogether, as an unnecessary complication. It can be of some help to the more skilled, intuitive reader, but even then its significance should be muted. In most cases, it is safe to assume that reversed cards indicate the way circumstances appear to us, while upright cards indicate the way they appear to the soul. A second common meaning is that reversed cards indicate problems which must be changed by us, while upright cards point to opportunities we might miss unless we are ready to act on them.

Having laid out the 10 cards, the one remaining step is to interpret them. It is not within the scope of this brief introduction to reveal the rich complexity of each of the symbols in the Tarot. I have provided a complete structure for interpreting the Tarot in my book **Exploring the Tarot,** and hope that you would use this resource in conjuction with **The Tarot Journal.** The important point to remember here is that the 10 cards of your spread do not represent 10 separate answers to your inquiry. They represent 10 pieces of a single answer, and need to be interpreted together, as a single, unified message, in order to make sense.

The process of recording your interpretation begins on the left-hand page of your journal entry. Take the time to count the number of cards in the Major Arcana and each suit and record them in the space provided. Also examine numerological parallels. If the sixth card is the Two of Pentacles and the seventh card is Judgment, the 20th card in the Major Arcana, then there is a numerological relationship between these two cards (20 = 2 + 0 = 2). Draw a line between these two cards on the diagram on the left-hand page of your record. Make a note, if you desire, that your confusion stems from not being able to see how your own attitudes and thoughts interact with higher forces to precipitate your problem or challenge.

Once you have made all of the appropriate notes on the left-hand page (including recording the name and number of each card in its appropriate location), then your work of interpretation can shift to the right-hand page of your record, where you jot down specific notes of interpretation relating to your question. In doing this, it is not necessary to start with the first card and end with the 10th. If the fifth card stands out most dramatically to you, begin there, and relate the rest of the cards to it. You can fill in your record in any order you prefer.

Some might ask, "Do we even need a question? Doesn't the Tarot know better than we what we ought to be asking?" The answers are yes and no. Yes, we need a question. And no, the Tarot does not know what we need to know. Our Higher Intelligence might, but the Tarot does not. The Tarot is a structure of intelligence very much like a computer, but without the hardware. A computer can do wonderful tasks, but only when we give it specific missions to perform. The same is true with the Tarot. Our question assigns it the task it will perform. Our task is to interpret it.

In this light, however, it is helpful to understand that the process of formulating the question should be a deliberate one. The Tarot will answer the question we ask, not what we meant to ask. So phrase the question carefully. And once it is phrased, be sure to write it down, in the space provided. Unless you write it down and refer back to it frequently, there will be an immense temptation to alter the original question to fit the answer you want to hear!

As you interpret the spread, also keep in mind that all of these cards represent divine forces and possibilities. No card is inherently bad or evil, and no card is automatically good. This applies even to The Devil, a card that portrays the divine force that generates schism and destruction. The appearance of The Devil in a spread might indicate that you are succumbing to temptation—but it might also indicate that the decks are being cleaned of a lot of garbage, giving you a new opportunity to get on with your life.

As always, remember that the answer you seek lies in 10 cards interpreted together, not in any one or two cards that happen to startle you.

For this reason, also take care not just to interpret the cards that appeal to you, while glossing over the ones that are harder to interpret—or seem dangerous to you. Such cards are likely to be the most pregnant with meaning and insight.

If you are determined to become skilled in the use of The Tarot, you might want to consider using more than one Journal. It might make more sense to have a separate Journal for each kind of question you tend to ask:

• Questions of self-examination. (How do I prevent myself from being happy? What blind spots do I need to remove? How can I best heal myself?)

• Questions about relationships. (How can I improve the closeness and intimacy of a relationship? Why do I feel betrayed by the actions of a friend?)

• Questions about parenting. (What's the best way to teach kids about sex? About drugs? What is the proper role of the parent toward the child?)

• Career questions. (What are the major opportunities for me at work this coming week? How does my work relate to the needs of humanity?)

• Questions that explore the inner dimensions of life and meaning. (What is the esoteric meaning of family? What is the best way to deal with the death of a loved one? What does it mean to think?)

• National and international questions. (What is the impact of pessimism on human thinking? How does the Spirit of America guide us?)

• Questions about contacting the soul. (What spiritual qualities do I need to add to my self-expression? How best can I build the antahkarana in this lifetime? What is the lesson of the spiritual crises I have undergone?)

In this way, it would be much easier to look for meaningful patterns as you fill each book with readings.

—Carl Japikse

The Tarot Journal

Date:
Question:

___

3.

10.

5.   1.   6.   9.

2.   8.

Majors:
Swords:
Rods: 4.   7.
Cups:
Pentacles:

Indexed To:

1.
2.
3.
4.
5.
6.
7.
8.
9.
10.

Date:
Question: _____
_____

3.

10.

5.

1.

6.

9.

2.

8.

Majors:
Swords:
Rods:
Cups:
Pentacles:

4.

7.

Indexed To:

1.

2.

3.

4.

5.

6.

7.

8.

9.

10.

Date:
Question:

```
        ┌─────┐                    ┌─────┐
        │ 3.  │                    │ 10. │
        │     │                    │     │
        │     │                    │     │
        │     │                    │     │
        └─────┘                    └─────┘

┌─────┐ ┌─────┐        ┌─────┐     ┌─────┐
│ 5.  │ │ 1.  │        │ 6.  │     │ 9.  │
│     │ │     │        │     │     │     │
│     │ │     │        │     │     │     │
└─────┘ └─────┘        └─────┘     └─────┘

        ┌───────────────┐          ┌─────┐
        │ 2.            │          │ 8.  │
        │               │          │     │
        └───────────────┘          │     │
                                   └─────┘
        ┌─────┐
        │ 4.  │
Majors: │     │
Swords: │     │                    ┌─────┐
Rods:   │     │                    │ 7.  │
Cups:   │     │                    │     │
Pentacles: │ │                    │     │
        └─────┘                    └─────┘
        Indexed To:
```

1.

2.

3.

4.

5.

6.

7.

8.

9.

10.

Date:
Question:

[3.]

[10.]

[5.] [1.] [6.] [9.]

[2.]

[8.]

[4.]

Majors:
Swords:
Rods: [7.]
Cups:
Pentacles:

Indexed To:

1.

2.

3.

4.

5.

6.

7.

8.

9.

10.

Date:
Question: _____
_____
_____

```
        [ 3. ]              [ 10. ]

[ 5. ]  [ 1. ]  [ 6. ]      [ 9. ]

        [ 2.    ]           [ 8. ]

        [ 4. ]
Majors:
Swords:
Rods:                       [ 7. ]
Cups:
Pentacles:
              Indexed To:
```

1.

2.

3.

4.

5.

6.

7.

8.

9.

10.

Date:
Question:
_____
_____
_____

3.

10.

5.

1.

6.

9.

2.

8.

4.

Majors:
Swords:
Rods:
Cups:
Pentacles:

7.

Indexed To:

1.

2.

3.

4.

5.

6.

7.

8.

9.

10.

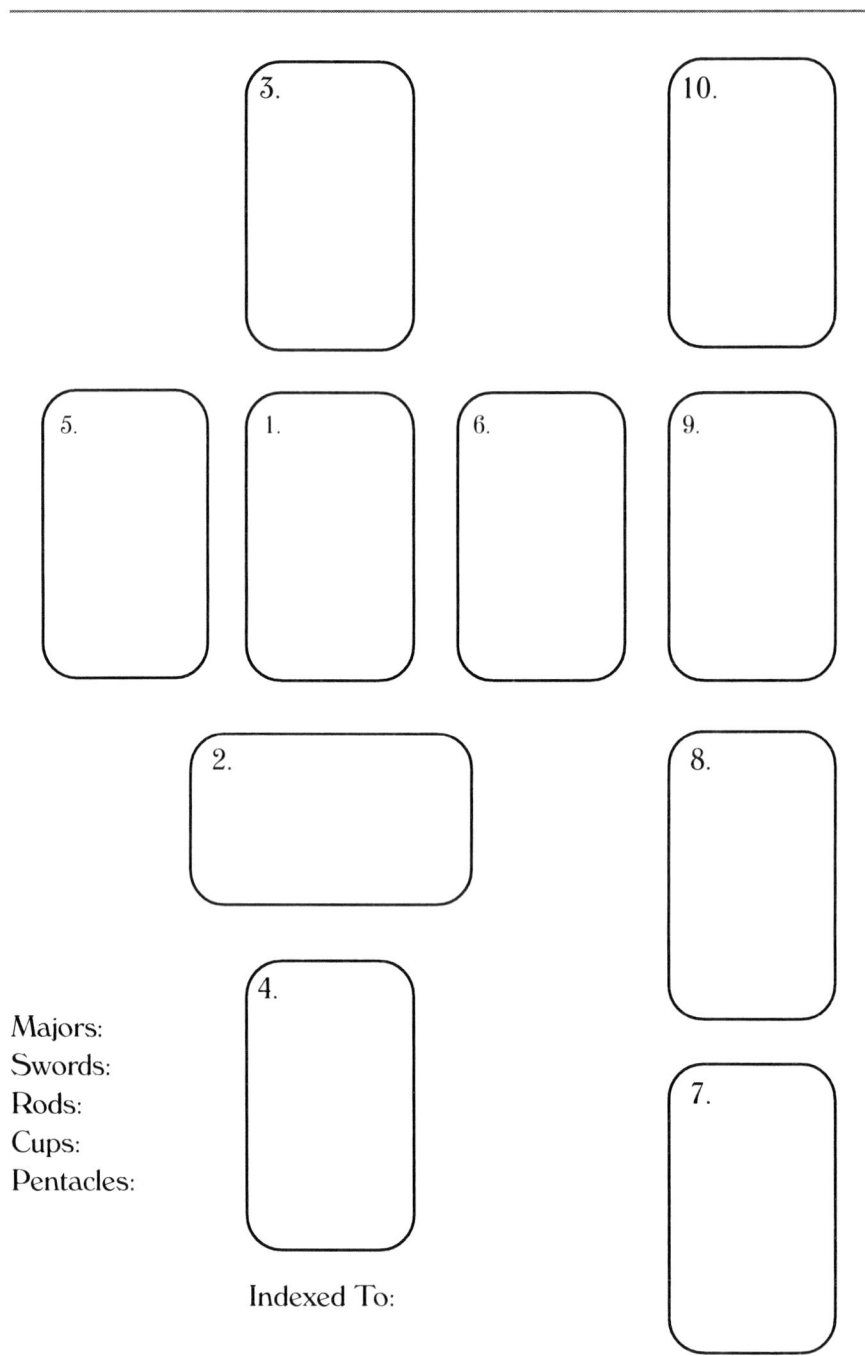

Date:
Question:
_____
_____

3.

10.

5.

1.

6.

9.

2.

8.

Majors:
Swords:
Rods:
Cups:
Pentacles:

4.

7.

Indexed To:

1.

2.

3.

4.

5.

6.

7.

8.

9.

10.

Date:
Question:
_____
_____

3.

10.

5.

1.

6.

9.

2.

8.

Majors:
Swords:
Rods:
Cups:
Pentacles:

4.

7.

Indexed To:

1.

2.

3.

4.

5.

6.

7.

8.

9.

10.

Date:
Question: _____
_____

```
          ┌─────┐                    ┌─────┐
          │ 3.  │                    │ 10. │
          │     │                    │     │
          │     │                    │     │
          │     │                    │     │
          └─────┘                    └─────┘

┌─────┐   ┌─────┐   ┌─────┐   ┌─────┐
│ 5.  │   │ 1.  │   │ 6.  │   │ 9.  │
│     │   │     │   │     │   │     │
│     │   │     │   │     │   │     │
└─────┘   └─────┘   └─────┘   └─────┘

          ┌───────────────┐          ┌─────┐
          │ 2.            │          │ 8.  │
          │               │          │     │
          └───────────────┘          │     │
                                     └─────┘

          ┌─────┐                    ┌─────┐
Majors:   │ 4.  │                    │ 7.  │
Swords:   │     │                    │     │
Rods:     │     │                    │     │
Cups:     │     │                    │     │
Pentacles:│     │                    │     │
          └─────┘                    └─────┘
          Indexed To:
```

1.

2.

3.

4.

5.

6.

7.

8.

9.

10.

Date:
Question:
_____
_____
_____

3.

10.

5.

1.

6.

9.

2.

8.

Majors:
Swords:
Rods:
Cups:
Pentacles:

4.

7.

Indexed To:

1.

2.

3.

4.

5.

6.

7.

8.

9.

10.

Date:
Question: _____
_____

| 3. | | | 10. |

| 5. | 1. | 6. | 9. |

| | 2. | | 8. |

Majors:
Swords:
Rods: | 4. | | 7. |
Cups:
Pentacles:

Indexed To:

36

1.

2.

3.

4.

5.

6.

7.

8.

9.

10.

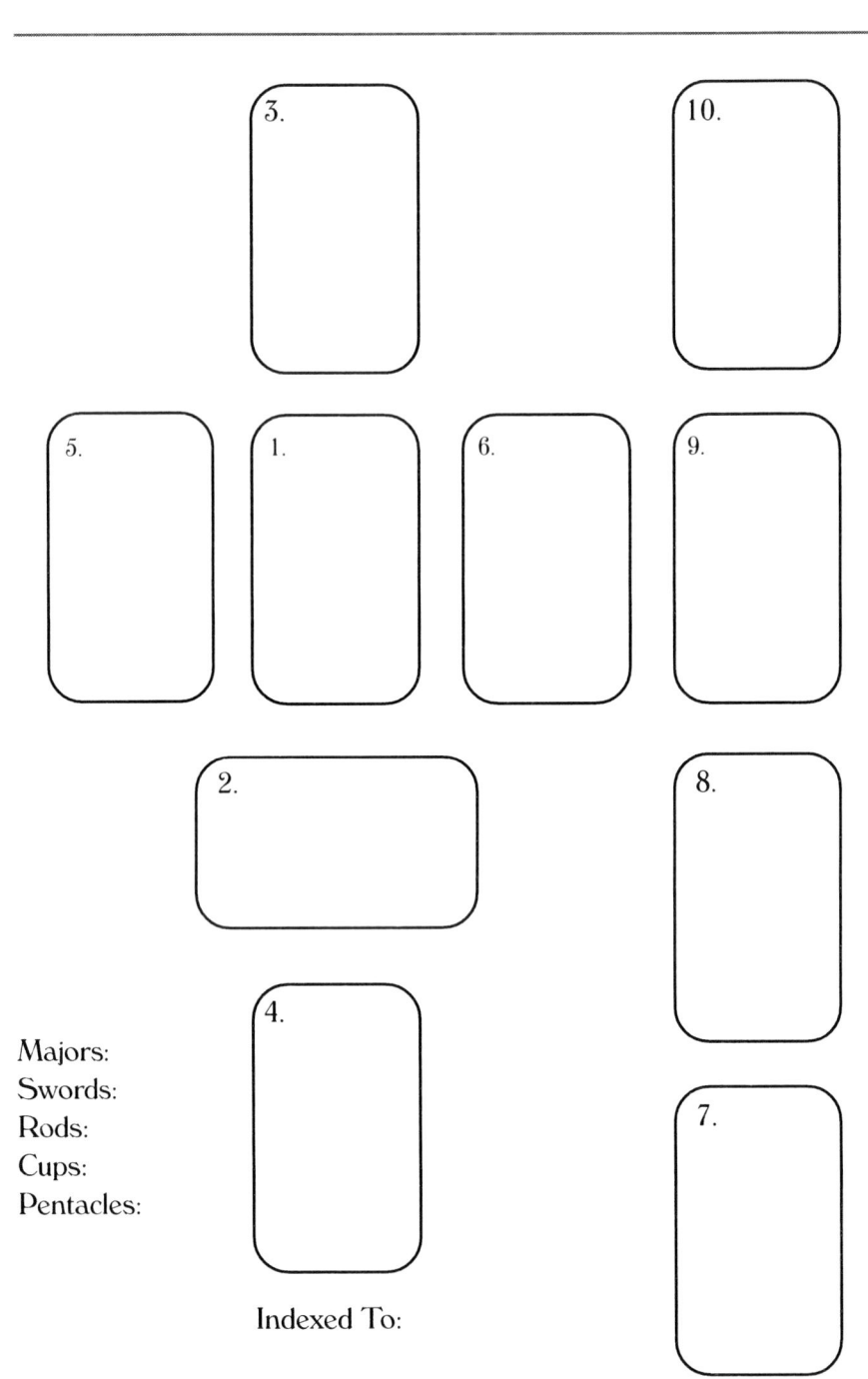

Date:
Question: _____

_____

[3.]   [10.]

[5.]   [1.]   [6.]   [9.]

        [2.]   [8.]

Majors:
Swords:
Rods: [4.]   [7.]
Cups:
Pentacles:

        Indexed To:

1.

2.

3.

4.

5.

6.

7.

8.

9.

10.

Date:
Question: _____
_____
_____

3.

10.

5.

1.

6.

9.

2.

8.

Majors:
Swords:
Rods:
Cups:
Pentacles:

4.

7.

Indexed To:

1.
2.
3.
4.
5.
6.
7.
8.
9.
10.

Date:
Question:

```
        ┌─────┐              ┌─────┐
        │ 3.  │              │ 10. │
        │     │              │     │
        │     │              │     │
        └─────┘              └─────┘

┌─────┐ ┌─────┐    ┌─────┐  ┌─────┐
│ 5.  │ │ 1.  │    │ 6.  │  │ 9.  │
│     │ │     │    │     │  │     │
└─────┘ └─────┘    └─────┘  └─────┘

        ┌──────────────┐     ┌─────┐
        │ 2.           │     │ 8.  │
        │              │     │     │
        └──────────────┘     └─────┘
```

Majors:
Swords:
Rods:
Cups:
Pentacles:

4.

7.

Indexed To:

1.

2.

3.

4.

5.

6.

7.

8.

9.

10.

Date:
Question:

3.

10.

5.

1.

6.

9.

2.

8.

Majors:
Swords:
Rods:
Cups:
Pentacles:

4.

7.

Indexed To:

1.

2.

3.

4.

5.

6.

7.

8.

9.

10.

Date:
Question: _____
_____
_____

```
        ┌─────┐                    ┌─────┐
        │ 3.  │                    │ 10. │
        │     │                    │     │
        │     │                    │     │
        └─────┘                    └─────┘

┌─────┐ ┌─────┐      ┌─────┐      ┌─────┐
│ 5.  │ │ 1.  │      │ 6.  │      │ 9.  │
│     │ │     │      │     │      │     │
└─────┘ └─────┘      └─────┘      └─────┘

        ┌───────────┐              ┌─────┐
        │ 2.        │              │ 8.  │
        │           │              │     │
        └───────────┘              │     │
                                   └─────┘
        ┌─────┐
Majors: │ 4.  │
Swords: │     │                    ┌─────┐
Rods:   │     │                    │ 7.  │
Cups:   │     │                    │     │
Pentacles:│   │                    │     │
        └─────┘                    └─────┘
        Indexed To:
```

1.

2.

3.

4.

5.

6.

7.

8.

9.

10.

Date:
Question:

3.

10.

5.

1.

6.

9.

2.

8.

Majors:
Swords:
Rods:
Cups:
Pentacles:

4.

7.

Indexed To:

1.

2.

3.

4.

5.

6.

7.

8.

9.

10.

Date:
Question:
_____
_____

```
        ┌─────┐                      ┌─────┐
        │ 3.  │                      │ 10. │
        │     │                      │     │
        │     │                      │     │
        │     │                      │     │
        └─────┘                      └─────┘

┌─────┐ ┌─────┐      ┌─────┐         ┌─────┐
│ 5.  │ │ 1.  │      │ 6.  │         │ 9.  │
│     │ │     │      │     │         │     │
│     │ │     │      │     │         │     │
│     │ │     │      │     │         │     │
└─────┘ └─────┘      └─────┘         └─────┘

        ┌──────────────┐             ┌─────┐
        │ 2.           │             │ 8.  │
        │              │             │     │
        └──────────────┘             │     │
                                     │     │
                                     └─────┘
        ┌─────┐
        │ 4.  │                      ┌─────┐
Majors: │     │                      │ 7.  │
Swords: │     │                      │     │
Rods:   │     │                      │     │
Cups:   │     │                      │     │
Pentacles: └─────┘                   └─────┘

        Indexed To:
```

Majors:
Swords:
Rods:
Cups:
Pentacles:

Indexed To:

50

1.

2.

3.

4.

5.

6.

7.

8.

9.

10.

Date:
Question: _____
_____

3.

10.

5.

1.

6.

9.

2.

8.

Majors:
Swords:
Rods:
Cups:
Pentacles:

4.

7.

Indexed To:

1.

2.

3.

4.

5.

6.

7.

8.

9.

10.

Date:
Question: _____
_____

3.

10.

5.   1.   6.   9.

2.   8.

4.

Majors:
Swords:
Rods: 7.
Cups:
Pentacles:

Indexed To:

1.
2.
3.
4.
5.
6.
7.
8.
9.
10.

Date:
Question: _____
_____
_____

```
         3.                    10.




5.    1.       6.      9.



      2.                8.



Majors:   4.
Swords:
Rods:          7.
Cups:
Pentacles:


      Indexed To:
```

1.
2.
3.
4.
5.
6.
7.
8.
9.
10.

Date:
Question: _____

```
        ┌─────┐                    ┌─────┐
        │ 3.  │                    │ 10. │
        │     │                    │     │
        │     │                    │     │
        │     │                    │     │
        └─────┘                    └─────┘

┌─────┐ ┌─────┐      ┌─────┐      ┌─────┐
│ 5.  │ │ 1.  │      │ 6.  │      │ 9.  │
│     │ │     │      │     │      │     │
│     │ │     │      │     │      │     │
└─────┘ └─────┘      └─────┘      └─────┘

        ┌───────────────┐          ┌─────┐
        │ 2.            │          │ 8.  │
        │               │          │     │
        └───────────────┘          │     │
                                   └─────┘
        ┌─────┐
        │ 4.  │
Majors: │     │
Swords: │     │                    ┌─────┐
Rods:   │     │                    │ 7.  │
Cups:   │     │                    │     │
Pentacles:    │                    │     │
        └─────┘                    └─────┘

        Indexed To:
```

1.

2.

3.

4.

5.

6.

7.

8.

9.

10.

Date:

Question: _____

_____

```
          ┌─────┐                    ┌─────┐
          │ 3.  │                    │ 10. │
          │     │                    │     │
          │     │                    │     │
          └─────┘                    └─────┘

┌─────┐   ┌─────┐   ┌─────┐   ┌─────┐
│ 5.  │   │ 1.  │   │ 6.  │   │ 9.  │
│     │   │     │   │     │   │     │
│     │   │     │   │     │   │     │
└─────┘   └─────┘   └─────┘   └─────┘

          ┌─────────┐              ┌─────┐
          │ 2.      │              │ 8.  │
          │         │              │     │
          └─────────┘              │     │
                                   └─────┘
Majors:   ┌─────┐
Swords:   │ 4.  │                  ┌─────┐
Rods:     │     │                  │ 7.  │
Cups:     │     │                  │     │
Pentacles:│     │                  │     │
          └─────┘                  └─────┘

          Indexed To:
```

1.

2.

3.

4.

5.

6.

7.

8.

9.

10.

Date:
Question: _____
_____
_____

```
        ┌─────┐                ┌─────┐
        │ 3.  │                │ 10. │
        │     │                │     │
        │     │                │     │
        └─────┘                └─────┘
┌─────┐ ┌─────┐ ┌─────┐ ┌─────┐
│ 5.  │ │ 1.  │ │ 6.  │ │ 9.  │
│     │ │     │ │     │ │     │
└─────┘ └─────┘ └─────┘ └─────┘
        ┌─────────┐            ┌─────┐
        │ 2.      │            │ 8.  │
        └─────────┘            │     │
                               └─────┘
        ┌─────┐
Majors: │ 4.  │
Swords: │     │                ┌─────┐
Rods:   │     │                │ 7.  │
Cups:   │     │                │     │
Pentacles: └──┘                └─────┘
        Indexed To:
```

62

1.

2.

3.

4.

5.

6.

7.

8.

9.

10.

Date:
Question: _____
_____
_____

```
        ┌─────┐                    ┌─────┐
        │ 3.  │                    │ 10. │
        │     │                    │     │
        │     │                    │     │
        │     │                    │     │
        └─────┘                    └─────┘

┌─────┐ ┌─────┐      ┌─────┐      ┌─────┐
│ 5.  │ │ 1.  │      │ 6.  │      │ 9.  │
│     │ │     │      │     │      │     │
│     │ │     │      │     │      │     │
│     │ │     │      │     │      │     │
└─────┘ └─────┘      └─────┘      └─────┘

        ┌───────────┐              ┌─────┐
        │ 2.        │              │ 8.  │
        │           │              │     │
        └───────────┘              │     │
                                   │     │
                                   └─────┘
        ┌─────┐
        │ 4.  │
Majors: │     │
Swords: │     │              ┌─────┐
Rods:   │     │              │ 7.  │
Cups:   │     │              │     │
Pentacles:    │              │     │
        │     │              │     │
        └─────┘              └─────┘
        Indexed To:
```

Majors:
Swords:
Rods:
Cups:
Pentacles:

Indexed To:

1.

2.

3.

4.

5.

6.

7.

8.

9.

10.

Date:
Question:

3.

10.

5.

1.

6.

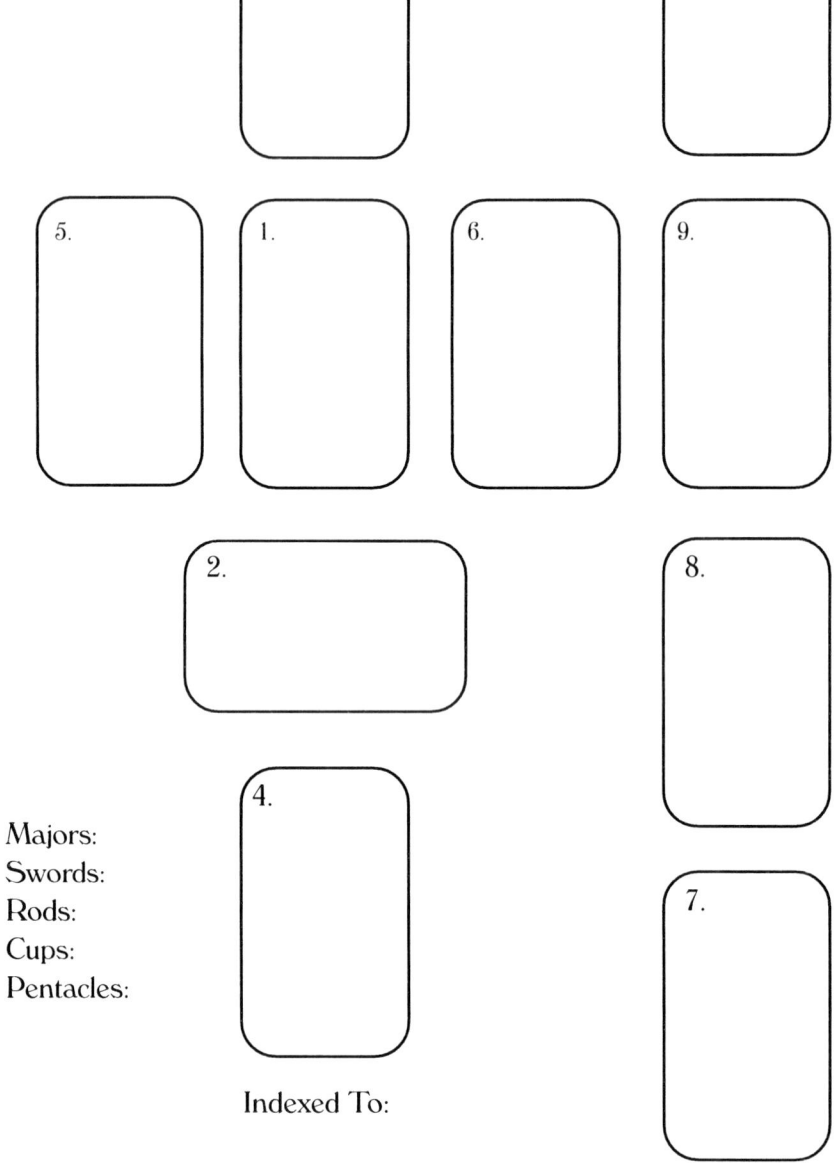

9.

2.

8.

Majors:
Swords:
Rods:
Cups:
Pentacles:

4.

7.

Indexed To:

1.

2.

3.

4.

5.

6.

7.

8.

9.

10.

Date:
Question: _____
_____

```
        [ 3. ]              [ 10. ]



[ 5. ]  [ 1. ]  [ 6. ]  [ 9. ]



        [ 2.      ]         [ 8. ]


Majors:  [ 4. ]
Swords:
Rods:                       [ 7. ]
Cups:
Pentacles:

        Indexed To:
```

1.

2.

3.

4.

5.

6.

7.

8.

9.

10.

Date:
Question: _____
_____
_____

| 3. | | | 10. |

| 5. | 1. | 6. | 9. |

| 2. | | 8. |

Majors:
Swords:
Rods: | 4. | | 7. |
Cups:
Pentacles:

Indexed To:

70

1.

2.

3.

4.

5.

6.

7.

8.

9.

10.

Date:
Question:

3.

10.

5.

1.

6.

9.

2.

8.

Majors:
Swords:
Rods:
Cups:
Pentacles:

4.

7.

Indexed To:

1.

2.

3.

4.

5.

6.

7.

8.

9.

10.

Date:
Question:

```
         ┌─────┐              ┌─────┐
         │ 3.  │              │ 10. │
         │     │              │     │
         │     │              │     │
         └─────┘              └─────┘

┌─────┐  ┌─────┐  ┌─────┐  ┌─────┐
│ 5.  │  │ 1.  │  │ 6.  │  │ 9.  │
│     │  │     │  │     │  │     │
└─────┘  └─────┘  └─────┘  └─────┘

         ┌──────────┐        ┌─────┐
         │ 2.       │        │ 8.  │
         │          │        │     │
         └──────────┘        └─────┘

Majors:  ┌─────┐
Swords:  │ 4.  │           ┌─────┐
Rods:    │     │           │ 7.  │
Cups:    │     │           │     │
Pentacles:└─────┘          └─────┘

         Indexed To:
```

Majors:
Swords:
Rods:
Cups:
Pentacles:

Indexed To:

74

1.
2.
3.
4.
5.
6.
7.
8.
9.
10.

Date:
Question: _____
_____
_____

```
        ┌─────┐                         ┌─────┐
        │ 3.  │                         │ 10. │
        │     │                         │     │
        │     │                         │     │
        │     │                         │     │
        └─────┘                         └─────┘

┌─────┐ ┌─────┐       ┌─────┐ ┌─────┐
│ 5.  │ │ 1.  │       │ 6.  │ │ 9.  │
│     │ │     │       │     │ │     │
│     │ │     │       │     │ │     │
└─────┘ └─────┘       └─────┘ └─────┘

        ┌───────────┐                   ┌─────┐
        │ 2.        │                   │ 8.  │
        │           │                   │     │
        └───────────┘                   │     │
                                        └─────┘

              ┌─────┐
              │ 4.  │
Majors:       │     │
Swords:       │     │            ┌─────┐
Rods:         │     │            │ 7.  │
Cups:         │     │            │     │
Pentacles:    └─────┘            │     │
                                 └─────┘
           Indexed To:
```

1.

2.

3.

4.

5.

6.

7.

8.

9.

10.

Date:
Question:

_____
_____
_____

| 3. | | | 10. |

| 5. | 1. | 6. | 9. |

| 2. | | 8. |

Majors:
Swords:
Rods: | 4. | | 7. |
Cups:
Pentacles:

Indexed To:

1.

2.

3.

4.

5.

6.

7.

8.

9.

10.

Date:
Question:

```
                  ┌─────┐              ┌─────┐
                  │ 3.  │              │ 10. │
                  │     │              │     │
                  │     │              │     │
                  └─────┘              └─────┘

   ┌─────┐    ┌─────┐    ┌─────┐    ┌─────┐
   │ 5.  │    │ 1.  │    │ 6.  │    │ 9.  │
   │     │    │     │    │     │    │     │
   └─────┘    └─────┘    └─────┘    └─────┘

              ┌──────────┐            ┌─────┐
              │ 2.       │            │ 8.  │
              │          │            │     │
              └──────────┘            └─────┘
```

              ┌─────┐
              │ 4. │
Majors: │   │
Swords: │   │   ┌─────┐
Rods: │   │   │ 7. │
Cups: │   │   │   │
Pentacles: └─────┘   └─────┘

              Indexed To:

80

1.

2.

3.

4.

5.

6.

7.

8.

9.

10.

Date:
Question: _____
_____

3.

10.

5. 1. 6. 9.

2. 8.

Majors:
Swords:
Rods: 4. 7.
Cups:
Pentacles:

Indexed To:

1.

2.

3.

4.

5.

6.

7.

8.

9.

10.

Date:
Question:

3.

10.

5.

1.

6.

9.

2.

8.

Majors:
Swords:
Rods:
Cups:
Pentacles:

4.

7.

Indexed To:

1.

2.

3.

4.

5.

6.

7.

8.

9.

10.

Date:
Question: _____
_____
_____

```
        ┌─────┐                    ┌─────┐
        │ 3.  │                    │ 10. │
        │     │                    │     │
        │     │                    │     │
        │     │                    │     │
        └─────┘                    └─────┘

┌─────┐ ┌─────┐      ┌─────┐       ┌─────┐
│ 5.  │ │ 1.  │      │ 6.  │       │ 9.  │
│     │ │     │      │     │       │     │
│     │ │     │      │     │       │     │
│     │ │     │      │     │       │     │
└─────┘ └─────┘      └─────┘       └─────┘

        ┌─────────┐                ┌─────┐
        │ 2.      │                │ 8.  │
        │         │                │     │
        └─────────┘                │     │
                                   │     │
                                   └─────┘
        ┌─────┐
        │ 4.  │
Majors: │     │
Swords: │     │                    ┌─────┐
Rods:   │     │                    │ 7.  │
Cups:   │     │                    │     │
Pentacles: │  │                    │     │
        └─────┘                    │     │
      Indexed To:                  └─────┘
```

1.

2.

3.

4.

5.

6.

7.

8.

9.

10.

Date:

Question: _____

_____

```
         ┌─────┐                    ┌─────┐
         │ 3.  │                    │ 10. │
         │     │                    │     │
         │     │                    │     │
         │     │                    │     │
         └─────┘                    └─────┘
┌─────┐  ┌─────┐  ┌─────┐  ┌─────┐
│ 5.  │  │ 1.  │  │ 6.  │  │ 9.  │
│     │  │     │  │     │  │     │
│     │  │     │  │     │  │     │
└─────┘  └─────┘  └─────┘  └─────┘
         ┌───────────┐              ┌─────┐
         │ 2.        │              │ 8.  │
         │           │              │     │
         └───────────┘              │     │
                                    └─────┘
Majors:  ┌─────┐
Swords:  │ 4.  │
Rods:    │     │                    ┌─────┐
Cups:    │     │                    │ 7.  │
Pentacles:│    │                    │     │
         └─────┘                    │     │
                                    └─────┘
         Indexed To:
```

88

1.

2.

3.

4.

5.

6.

7.

8.

9.

10.

Date:
Question:

3.

10.

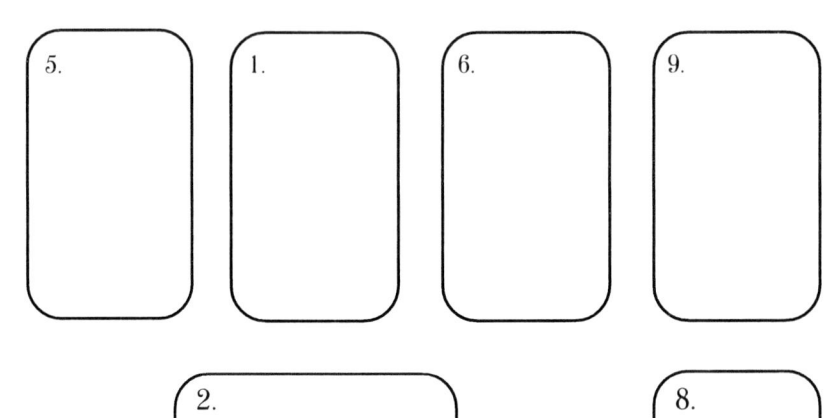

5.

1.

6.

9.

2.

8.

Majors:
Swords:
Rods:
Cups:
Pentacles:

4.

7.

Indexed To:

1.

2.

3.

4.

5.

6.

7.

8.

9.

10.

Date:
Question:
_____
_____

3.

10.

5.

1.

6.

9.

2.

8.

Majors:
Swords:
Rods:
Cups:
Pentacles:

4.

7.

Indexed To:

1.

2.

3.

4.

5.

6.

7.

8.

9.

10.

Date:
Question: _____
_____

3.

10.

5.   1.   6.   9.

2.   8.

Majors:
Swords:
Rods: 4.   7.
Cups:
Pentacles:

Indexed To:

1.

2.

3.

4.

5.

6.

7.

8.

9.

10.

Date:
Question: _____
_____
_____

| 3. | | 10. |

| 5. | 1. | 6. | 9. |

| 2. | | 8. |

Majors:
Swords:
Rods: 7.
Cups:
Pentacles:

4.

Indexed To:

96

1.

2.

3.

4.

5.

6.

7.

8.

9.

10.

Date:
Question: _____
_____
_____

```
        ┌─────┐              ┌─────┐
        │ 3.  │              │ 10. │
        │     │              │     │
        │     │              │     │
        │     │              │     │
        └─────┘              └─────┘

┌─────┐ ┌─────┐     ┌─────┐  ┌─────┐
│ 5.  │ │ 1.  │     │ 6.  │  │ 9.  │
│     │ │     │     │     │  │     │
│     │ │     │     │     │  │     │
│     │ │     │     │     │  │     │
└─────┘ └─────┘     └─────┘  └─────┘

        ┌───────────────┐    ┌─────┐
        │ 2.            │    │ 8.  │
        │               │    │     │
        └───────────────┘    │     │
                             │     │
                             └─────┘
        ┌─────┐
        │ 4.  │              ┌─────┐
Majors: │     │              │ 7.  │
Swords: │     │              │     │
Rods:   │     │              │     │
Cups:   │     │              │     │
Pentacles:                   └─────┘
        └─────┘
        Indexed To:
```

1.

2.

3.

4.

5.

6.

7.

8.

9.

10.

Date:
Question: _____
_____
_____

3.

10.

5.

1.

6.

9.

2.

8.

Majors:
Swords:
Rods:
Cups:
Pentacles:

4.

7.

Indexed To:

1.

2.

3.

4.

5.

6.

7.

8.

9.

10.

Date:
Question:

3.

10.

5.   1.   6.   9.

2.   8.

Majors:
Swords:
Rods: 4.   7.
Cups:
Pentacles:

Indexed To:

1.

2.

3.

4.

5.

6.

7.

8.

9.

10.

Date:
Question:
___

3.

10.

5.   1.   6.   9.

2.   8.

Majors:
Swords: 4.
Rods: 7.
Cups:
Pentacles:

Indexed To:

1.

2.

3.

4.

5.

6.

7.

8.

9.

10.

Date:

Question:
_____
_____

```
          ┌─────┐              ┌─────┐
          │ 3.  │              │ 10. │
          │     │              │     │
          │     │              │     │
          └─────┘              └─────┘

  ┌───┐   ┌─────┐   ┌─────┐   ┌─────┐
  │5. │   │ 1.  │   │ 6.  │   │ 9.  │
  │   │   │     │   │     │   │     │
  └───┘   └─────┘   └─────┘   └─────┘

          ┌─────────┐          ┌─────┐
          │ 2.      │          │ 8.  │
          └─────────┘          │     │
                               └─────┘
          ┌─────┐
          │ 4.  │              ┌─────┐
Majors:   │     │              │ 7.  │
Swords:   │     │              │     │
Rods:     │     │              │     │
Cups:     │     │              │     │
Pentacles:│     │              └─────┘
          └─────┘
          Indexed To:
```

Majors:
Swords:
Rods:
Cups:
Pentacles:

Indexed To:

1.

2.

3.

4.

5.

6.

7.

8.

9.

10.

Date:
Question:

3.

10.

5.

1.

6.

9.

2.

8.

Majors:
Swords:
Rods:
Cups:
Pentacles:

4.

7.

Indexed To:

1.

2.

3.

4.

5.

6.

7.

8.

9.

10.

Date:
Question:
_____
_____
_____

3.

10.

5.

1.

6.

9.

2.

8.

Majors:
Swords:
Rods:
Cups:
Pentacles:

4.

7.

Indexed To:

110

1.

2.

3.

4.

5.

6.

7.

8.

9.

10.

Date:
Question: _____
_____
_____

3.

10.

5.

1.

6.

9.

2.

8.

Majors:
Swords:
Rods:
Cups:
Pentacles:

4.

7.

Indexed To:

1.
2.
3.
4.
5.
6.
7.
8.
9.
10.

Date:
Question:
_____
_____
_____

3.

10.

5.

1.

6.

9.

2.

8.

Majors:
Swords:
Rods:
Cups:
Pentacles:

4.

7.

Indexed To:

1.

2.

3.

4.

5.

6.

7.

8.

9.

10.

Date:
Question:

```
                3.                    10.



5.        1.        6.        9.



        2.                    8.



Majors:
Swords:           4.
Rods:                        7.
Cups:
Pentacles:


            Indexed To:
```

1.
2.
3.
4.
5.
6.
7.
8.
9.
10.

Date:
Question:
_____
_____
_____

```
        ┌─────┐              ┌─────┐
        │ 3.  │              │ 10. │
        │     │              │     │
        │     │              │     │
        └─────┘              └─────┘

┌─────┐ ┌─────┐ ┌─────┐ ┌─────┐
│ 5.  │ │ 1.  │ │ 6.  │ │ 9.  │
│     │ │     │ │     │ │     │
└─────┘ └─────┘ └─────┘ └─────┘

        ┌─────────┐          ┌─────┐
        │ 2.      │          │ 8.  │
        │         │          │     │
        └─────────┘          └─────┘

                ┌─────┐
                │ 4.  │      ┌─────┐
Majors:         │     │      │ 7.  │
Swords:         │     │      │     │
Rods:           │     │      │     │
Cups:           │     │      └─────┘
Pentacles:      └─────┘
                Indexed To:
```

1.
2.
3.
4.
5.
6.
7.
8.
9.
10.

Date:
Question: _____
_____
_____

```
        ╭─────╮              ╭─────╮
        │ 3.  │              │ 10. │
        │     │              │     │
        │     │              │     │
        ╰─────╯              ╰─────╯

╭─────╮ ╭─────╮    ╭─────╮   ╭─────╮
│ 5.  │ │ 1.  │    │ 6.  │   │ 9.  │
│     │ │     │    │     │   │     │
╰─────╯ ╰─────╯    ╰─────╯   ╰─────╯

        ╭───────────╮        ╭─────╮
        │ 2.        │        │ 8.  │
        ╰───────────╯        │     │
                             ╰─────╯

        ╭─────╮
        │ 4.  │
Majors: │     │              ╭─────╮
Swords: │     │              │ 7.  │
Rods:   │     │              │     │
Cups:   │     │              │     │
Pentacles: ╰─────╯           ╰─────╯
        Indexed To:
```

1.

2.

3.

4.

5.

6.

7.

8.

9.

10.

Date:
Question:
_____
_____

3.

10.

5.

1.

6.

9.

2.

8.

Majors:
Swords:
Rods:
Cups:
Pentacles:

4.

7.

Indexed To:

1.
2.
3.
4.
5.
6.
7.
8.
9.
10.

Date:
Question:
_____
_____
_____

3.

10.

5.

1.

6.

9.

2.

8.

Majors:
Swords:
Rods:
Cups:
Pentacles:

4.

7.

Indexed To:

1.

2.

3.

4.

5.

6.

7.

8.

9.

10.

Date:
Question:
_____
_____

```
        ┌─────┐              ┌─────┐
        │ 3.  │              │ 10. │
        │     │              │     │
        │     │              │     │
        └─────┘              └─────┘

┌─────┐ ┌─────┐    ┌─────┐   ┌─────┐
│ 5.  │ │ 1.  │    │ 6.  │   │ 9.  │
│     │ │     │    │     │   │     │
└─────┘ └─────┘    └─────┘   └─────┘

        ┌───────────┐         ┌─────┐
        │    2.     │         │ 8.  │
        └───────────┘         │     │
                              └─────┘
        ┌─────┐
        │ 4.  │
Majors: │     │
Swords: │     │               ┌─────┐
Rods:   │     │               │ 7.  │
Cups:   │     │               │     │
Pentacles: └──┘               └─────┘

        Indexed To:
```

1.

2.

3.

4.

5.

6.

7.

8.

9.

10.

Date:
Question:
_____
_____
_____

3.

10.

5.

1.

6.

9.

2.

8.

Majors:
Swords:
Rods:
Cups:
Pentacles:

4.

7.

Indexed To:

1.

2.

3.

4.

5.

6.

7.

8.

9.

10.

Date:
Question: _____
_____
_____

	3.		10.
5.	1.	6.	9.
	2.		8.
	4.		7.

Majors:
Swords:
Rods:
Cups:
Pentacles:

Indexed To:

130

1.

2.

3.

4.

5.

6.

7.

8.

9.

10.

Date:
Question: _____
_____
_____

| 3. | | | 10. |

| 5. | 1. | 6. | 9. |

| | 2. | | 8. |

Majors:
Swords: | 4. |
Rods:
Cups: | 7. |
Pentacles:

Indexed To:

1.
2.
3.
4.
5.
6.
7.
8.
9.
10.

Date:
Question:

3.

10.

5.   1.   6.   9.

2.   8.

Majors:
Swords:
Rods: 7.
Cups:
Pentacles:

4.

Indexed To:

1.

2.

3.

4.

5.

6.

7.

8.

9.

10.

Date:
Question:
___

3.

10.

5.

1.

6.

9.

2.

8.

Majors:
Swords:
Rods:
Cups:
Pentacles:

4.

7.

Indexed To:

1.

2.

3.

4.

5.

6.

7.

8.

9.

10.

Date:
Question:

```
┌─────┐           ┌─────┐
│ 3.  │           │ 10. │
│     │           │     │
│     │           │     │
└─────┘           └─────┘

┌───┐ ┌─────┐ ┌───┐ ┌───┐
│5. │ │ 1.  │ │6. │ │9. │
│   │ │     │ │   │ │   │
└───┘ └─────┘ └───┘ └───┘

      ┌───────┐       ┌───┐
      │  2.   │       │8. │
      └───────┘       │   │
                      └───┘
      ┌─────┐
Majors: │ 4.  │
Swords: │     │       ┌───┐
Rods:  │     │       │7. │
Cups:  │     │       │   │
Pentacles: └─────┘   └───┘
      Indexed To:
```

1.

2.

3.

4.

5.

6.

7.

8.

9.

10.

Date:
Question: _____
_____
_____

3.

10.

5.

1.

6.

9.

2.

8.

Majors:
Swords:
Rods:
Cups:
Pentacles:

4.

7.

Indexed To:

1.

2.

3.

4.

5.

6.

7.

8.

9.

10.

Date:
Question:

```
    3.              10.




5.     1.     6.     9.




    2.              8.



Majors:
Swords:  4.
Rods:           7.
Cups:
Pentacles:



        Indexed To:
```

1.

2.

3.

4.

5.

6.

7.

8.

9.

10.

Date:
Question: _____
_____
_____

3.

10.

5.

1.

6.

9.

2.

8.

Majors:
Swords:
Rods: 7.
Cups:
Pentacles:

4.

Indexed To:

1.

2.

3.

4.

5.

6.

7.

8.

9.

10.

Date:
Question:

___

3.

10.

5.   1.   6.   9.

2.   8.

Majors:
Swords: 4.
Rods: 7.
Cups:
Pentacles:

Indexed To:

1.

2.

3.

4.

5.

6.

7.

8.

9.

10.

Date:
Question:

```
   ┌─────┐                    ┌─────┐
   │ 3.  │                    │ 10. │
   │     │                    │     │
   │     │                    │     │
   └─────┘                    └─────┘

┌─────┐  ┌─────┐  ┌─────┐  ┌─────┐
│ 5.  │  │ 1.  │  │ 6.  │  │ 9.  │
│     │  │     │  │     │  │     │
└─────┘  └─────┘  └─────┘  └─────┘

         ┌─────────┐          ┌─────┐
         │ 2.      │          │ 8.  │
         └─────────┘          │     │
                              └─────┘
         ┌─────┐
Majors:  │ 4.  │
Swords:  │     │              ┌─────┐
Rods:    │     │              │ 7.  │
Cups:    │     │              │     │
Pentacles:│    │              └─────┘
         └─────┘

         Indexed To:
```

Majors:
Swords:
Rods:
Cups:
Pentacles:

Indexed To:

1.

2.

3.

4.

5.

6.

7.

8.

9.

10.

Date:
Question: _____
_____
_____

```
         ┌─────┐                    ┌─────┐
         │ 3.  │                    │ 10. │
         │     │                    │     │
         │     │                    │     │
         │     │                    │     │
         └─────┘                    └─────┘

┌─────┐  ┌─────┐  ┌─────┐  ┌─────┐
│ 5.  │  │ 1.  │  │ 6.  │  │ 9.  │
│     │  │     │  │     │  │     │
│     │  │     │  │     │  │     │
└─────┘  └─────┘  └─────┘  └─────┘

         ┌──────────┐                ┌─────┐
         │ 2.       │                │ 8.  │
         │          │                │     │
         └──────────┘                │     │
                                     └─────┘
         ┌─────┐
Majors:  │ 4.  │
Swords:  │     │                    ┌─────┐
Rods:    │     │                    │ 7.  │
Cups:    │     │                    │     │
Pentacles:│    │                    │     │
         └─────┘                    └─────┘
         Indexed To:
```

1.

2.

3.

4.

5.

6.

7.

8.

9.

10.

Date:
Question:

```
     3.              10.



5.      1.      6.      9.



        2.              8.



        4.
Majors:
Swords:
Rods:           7.
Cups:
Pentacles:


        Indexed To:
```

1.
2.
3.
4.
5.
6.
7.
8.
9.
10.

Date:
Question:

_____
_____
_____

[3.]   [10.]

[5.] [1.] [6.] [9.]

[2.]   [8.]

Majors:
Swords:
Rods: [4.]   [7.]
Cups:
Pentacles:

Indexed To:

1.

2.

3.

4.

5.

6.

7.

8.

9.

10.

Date:
Question:
_____
_____

```
        ┌─────┐              ┌─────┐
        │ 3.  │              │ 10. │
        │     │              │     │
        │     │              │     │
        └─────┘              └─────┘

┌─────┐ ┌─────┐ ┌─────┐ ┌─────┐
│ 5.  │ │ 1.  │ │ 6.  │ │ 9.  │
│     │ │     │ │     │ │     │
└─────┘ └─────┘ └─────┘ └─────┘

        ┌───────────┐        ┌─────┐
        │ 2.        │        │ 8.  │
        │           │        │     │
        └───────────┘        │     │
                             └─────┘
        ┌─────┐
Majors: │ 4.  │
Swords: │     │              ┌─────┐
Rods:   │     │              │ 7.  │
Cups:   │     │              │     │
Pentacles: │  │              │     │
        └─────┘              └─────┘

        Indexed To:
```

1.

2.

3.

4.

5.

6.

7.

8.

9.

10.

Date:
Question:
_____
_____
_____

3.

10.

5.

1.

6.

9.

2.

8.

Majors:
Swords:
Rods:
Cups:
Pentacles:

4.

7.

Indexed To:

1.

2.

3.

4.

5.

6.

7.

8.

9.

10.

Date:
Question:
_____
_____

3.

10.

5.

1.

6.

9.

2.

8.

Majors:
Swords:
Rods:
Cups:
Pentacles:

4.

7.

Indexed To:

1.

2.

3.

4.

5.

6.

7.

8.

9.

10.

Date:
Question:

_____

_____

```
        [ 3. ]              [ 10. ]


[ 5. ]  [ 1. ]  [ 6. ]  [ 9. ]


        [ 2. ]              [ 8. ]


Majors:  [ 4. ]
Swords:
Rods:                       [ 7. ]
Cups:
Pentacles:

        Indexed To:
```

1.

2.

3.

4.

5.

6.

7.

8.

9.

10.

Date:
Question:

3.

10.

5. 1. 6. 9.

2. 8.

Majors:
Swords:
Rods: 4. 7.
Cups:
Pentacles:

Indexed To:

1.

2.

3.

4.

5.

6.

7.

8.

9.

10.

Date:
Question: _____
_____
_____

[3.]   [10.]

[5.] [1.] [6.] [9.]

[2.]   [8.]

Majors:
Swords: [4.]
Rods: [7.]
Cups:
Pentacles:

Indexed To:

1.

2.

3.

4.

5.

6.

7.

8.

9.

10.

Date:
Question:
_____
_____
_____

3.

10.

5.

1.

6.

9.

2.

8.

Majors:
Swords:
Rods:
Cups:
Pentacles:

4.

7.

Indexed To:

168

1.
2.
3.
4.
5.
6.
7.
8.
9.
10.

Date:
Question:
===

```
    3.              10.



5.      1.      6.      9.




    2.              8.


            
Majors:     4.
Swords:
Rods:           7.
Cups:
Pentacles:


        Indexed To:
```

1.

2.

3.

4.

5.

6.

7.

8.

9.

10.

Date:
Question:

```
     3.              10.




5.    1.    6.    9.




      2.          8.




Majors:
Swords:        7.
Rods:    4.
Cups:
Pentacles:


      Indexed To:
```

1.

2.

3.

4.

5.

6.

7.

8.

9.

10.

Date:
Question: _____
_____

```
         ┌─────┐                    ┌─────┐
         │ 3.  │                    │ 10. │
         │     │                    │     │
         │     │                    │     │
         │     │                    │     │
         └─────┘                    └─────┘

┌─────┐  ┌─────┐        ┌─────┐     ┌─────┐
│ 5.  │  │ 1.  │        │ 6.  │     │ 9.  │
│     │  │     │        │     │     │     │
│     │  │     │        │     │     │     │
└─────┘  └─────┘        └─────┘     └─────┘

         ┌───────────────┐          ┌─────┐
         │ 2.            │          │ 8.  │
         │               │          │     │
         └───────────────┘          │     │
                                    │     │
                                    └─────┘
         ┌─────┐
         │ 4.  │
Majors:  │     │
Swords:  │     │          ┌─────┐
Rods:    │     │          │ 7.  │
Cups:    │     │          │     │
Pentacles:│    │          │     │
         └─────┘          │     │
                          └─────┘
         Indexed To:
```

174

1.

2.

3.

4.

5.

6.

7.

8.

9.

10.

OTHER BOOKS PUBLISHED BY ARIEL PRESS:

Exploring the Tarot
by Carl Japikse, $14.95

Active Meditation: The Western Tradition
by Robert R. Leichtman, M.D. & Carl Japikse, $19.95

Forces of the Zodiac: Companions of the Soul
by Robert R. Leichtman, M.D. & Carl Japikse, $19.99

Fear No Evil
by Robert R. Leichtman, M.D., $9.95

The Secrets of Dr. Taverner
by Dion Fortune, $10.95

Practical Mysticism
by Evelyn Underhill, $9.95

The Light Within Us
by Carl Japikse, $9.95

Working With Angels
by Robert R. Leichtman, M.D. & Carl Japikse, $7.95.

I Ching Line by Line (four books)
by Robert R. Leichtman, M.D. & Carl Japikse, $30.

To order, call toll free 1-800-336-7769